THEODORE ROOSEVELT SCHOOL

ESEA TITLE I-VI 1976

JUDI SIKES

A Spooky Story

Holt, Rinehart and Winston, Inc.
New York, Toronto, London, Sydney

Bill Martin Instant Reader

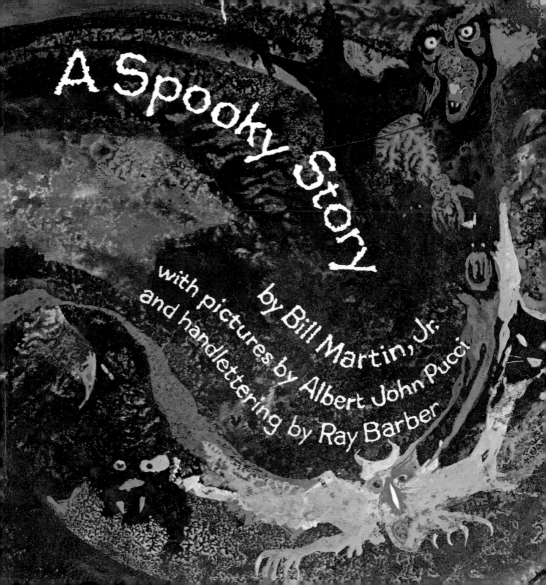

A Spooky Story

by Bill Martin, Jr.

with pictures by Albert John Pucci
and handlettering by Ray Barber

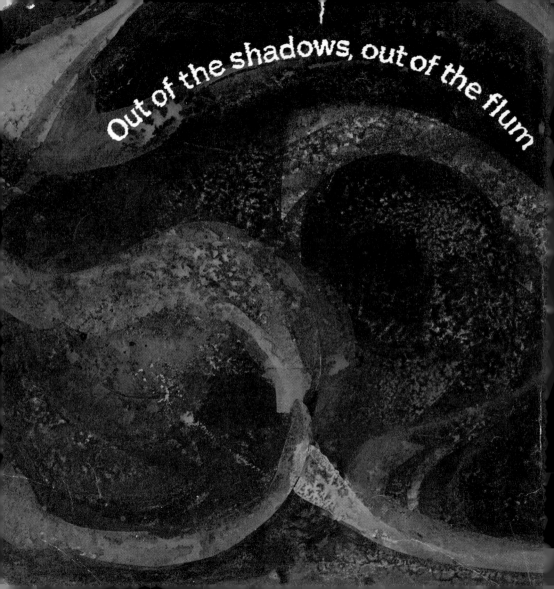

Out of the shadows, out of the flum

comes one creeping cat.

Out of the shadows, out of the flum

come two sweeping bats.

Out of the shadows, out of the flum

come three moaning gho

Out of the shadows, out of the flum

come four groaning goblins.

Out of the shadows, out of the flum

come five screaming vampires.

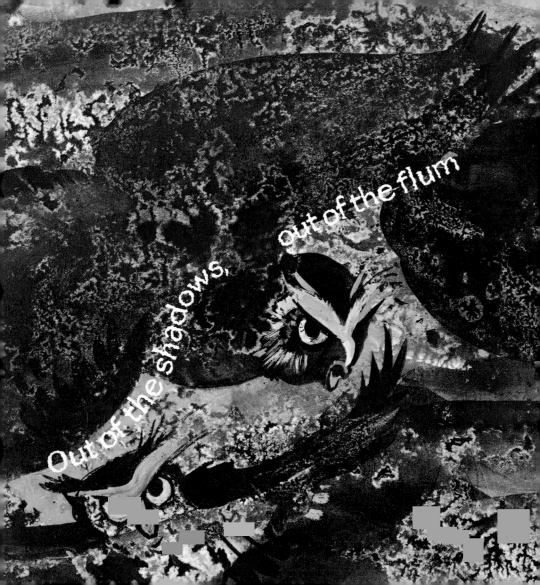

Out of the shadows, out of the flum

Come six screeching owls.

Out of the shadows, out of the flum

come seven shrieking witches.

Out of the shadows, out of the flum

come eight floating skeletons.

Out of the shadows, out of the flum

come nine howling werewolves.

Out of the shadows, out of the flum

Turning about, burning about,

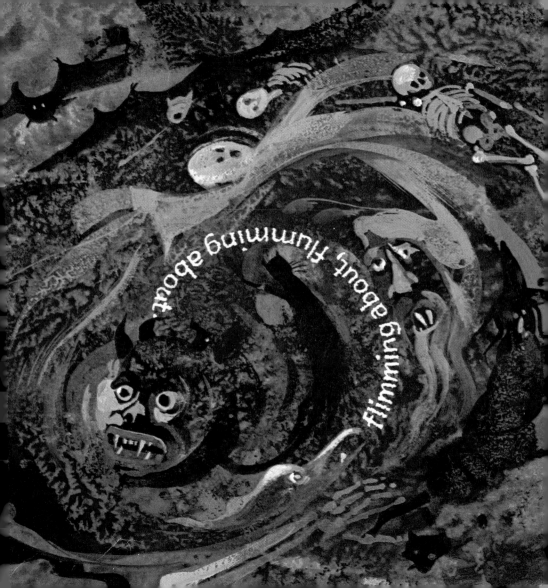

flimming about, flimming about,

Screaming about, sleaming about,

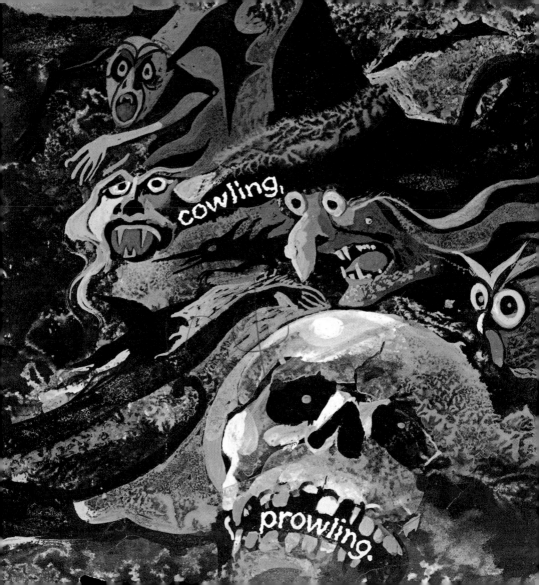

Then back into the flum they come.

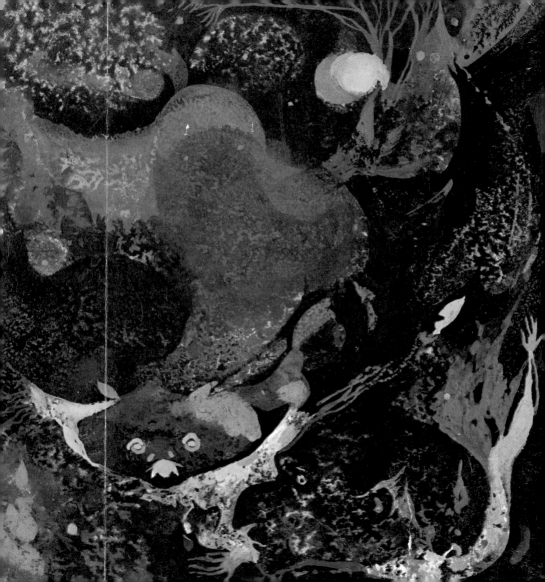